EARLY AMERICAN PATCHWORK PATTERNS

Full-Size Templates & Instructions for 12 Quilts

CAROL BELANGER GRAFTON

DOVER PUBLICATIONS, INC.
NEW YORK

Copyright © 1980 by Dover Publications, Inc.
All rights reserved under Pan American and International Copy-right Conventions.

Published in Canada by General Publishing Company, Ltd., 30 Lesmill Road, Don Mills, Toronto, Ontario.
Published in the United Kingdom by Constable and Company, Ltd., 10 Orange Street, London WC2H 7EG.

Early American Patchwork Patterns is a new work, first published by Dover Publications, Inc., in 1980.

Book design by Carol Belanger Grafton

International Standard Book Number: 0-486-23882-2
Library of Congress Catalog Card Number: 79-53932

Manufactured in the United States of America
Dover Publications, Inc.
31 East 2nd Street
Mineola, N.Y. 11501

INTRODUCTION

The twelve patchwork patterns in this book represent some of the loveliest and best-known early American quilts. Many of them are adaptations of quilts which are now seen only in museums and antique shops. I have not specified colors for the quilt blocks, but have simply indicated light, medium and dark. Possible color combinations are suggested by the illustrations on the covers of this book. You should feel free to use your own color scheme, making your blocks more or less complicated and more or less subtle in order to achieve quilts that are your personal creations.

These patterns selected for this collection provide challenges to both beginners and experts. Even more than the novices, those who have already made quilts by copying out designs onto cardboard will appreciate the convenience of the unusual feature of this collection—the carefully designed preprinted cardboard patterns or templates that make up the last half of this publication.

As the title indicates, this work is a collection of immediately useable patterns—not an instruction book on how to do patchwork; that subject is already well covered in numerous inexpensive books (one of the best of which is *The Standard Book of Quilt Making and Collecting* by Marguerite Ickis[1]), and limitations of space permit us only to sketch out the process in brief.

BEGINNING THE QUILT

Before cutting out the pieces for an entire quilt, always make one block of the pattern. This gives you a chance to double-check your pattern and to make certain that you like both the pattern and the color choices.

Cutting Out the Pattern Pieces

All of the pattern pieces used in making these quilts are given in actual-size patterns or templates printed on heavy-weight paper in the back of this book. Locate the designated template and carefully cut it out. Use this cardboard template to make your sample block. If you decide to make the entire quilt, you may want to mount your template on heavier cardboard, sandpaper or plastic.

It is important that all templates be cut out carefully because if they are not accurate, the patchwork pieces will not fit together. Use a pair of good-size sharp scissors, a single-edged razor blade or an X-acto knife. Be careful not to bend the fine corners of the triangles.

[1]A Dover paperback reprint (0-486-20582-7, 280pp.).

Kinds of Materials

At the beginning of each pattern, we indicate the amount of 36-inch-wide material you will need to complete a quilt of the specified dimensions. Of course, you are free to revise the proposed finished size of the quilt. This adjustment is accomplished by adding additional blocks or half-blocks to both the width and height.

The first rule to observe in selecting material for a quilt is to combine the same kinds of fabrics. For instance, linens and cottons go together, silks and satins, and so on. If you want to make a quilt that can be laundered, be sure that *all* the material used is washable and pre-shrunk and that the colors are fast.

For your convenience in sewing, select a soft material, not too closely woven. Closely woven cloth makes the needlework more difficult and is no stronger than thinner goods. Materials that are stiff because of being "treated" with a finish are also difficult to work with. In general, the following materials are good for patchwork quilts: gingham, percale, calico, shirting, broadcloth, and cotton-polyester blends.

Cutting the Fabric

Cutting is one of the most important steps in making your quilt. You must be accurate in order to have the pattern fit perfectly and to avoid wasting your materials. Have sharp scissors with blades at least 4 inches long. You will need a ruler for marking straight lines, and a pencil with hard lead to avoid blurry marks around the pattern.

Press all fabric to remove the wrinkles and crease marks. Check the grain line of the fabric carefully. Lengthwise threads should be parallel to the selvage and crosswise threads exactly perpendicular to the selvage to insure that the pieces will be correctly cut.

Take one of the templates and refer to the instructions to find out how many pieces of each fabric you will need to complete each block. After you have made your first sample block, multiply the number of blocks remaining to be completed by the number of pieces of each fabric required for one block and jot this information down in pencil on the pattern piece itself.

These templates are the exact size the patch will be after the sewing is done, and they have purposely been printed *without* the ¼-inch seam allowance. Lay the cardboard template on the wrong side of the fabric near the top edge of the material (but not on the selvage) placing it so as many straight sides of the pattern as possible are parallel to the crosswise and lengthwise grain of the fabric.

Trace around the cardboard with a well-sharpened, hard lead pencil. Now measure ¼ inch around this shape. Using a ruler, draw this second line. This is the line you will cut on. Now you will see that the first line (where you traced the template) is there to use as a guide for stitching. If the seam allowance is not perfect, this will not show; but the *sewing line* must be perfectly straight and true, or the pieces will not fit together into a perfectly shaped design.

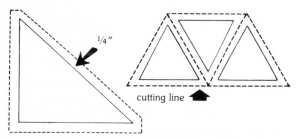

The broken line is the cutting line. The solid line is the seam line; match to the line on the next patch. Sewing is done on the solid line. The pieces can share a common cutting line.

Continue moving the template and tracing it on the fabric the required number of times, moving from left to right always keeping the straight sides parallel with the grain. As each piece is traced, add the ¼ inch around it before going on to the next piece. You will save fabric if you have the pieces share a common cutting line, but if this is confusing leave a narrow border or margin around each piece.

After you have traced the first pattern piece the required number of times, take one of the other pattern pieces that is to be cut from the same material, and trace it in a similar manner, again referring to the instructions printed with each quilt to determine the required number of pieces.

Run thread through center of patches according to shape and color. Knot at bottom and lift off patch from top as needed.

Carefully cut out all of the pieces of each color and then organize them according to shape and color. Most people find it convenient to keep the pieces of the same shape and color together by putting them in a pile and running a thread with a knot in one end through the center. Each piece is then lifted off as it is needed.

Sewing the Block

Before beginning to sew one block, lay out all of the pieces that will be needed for that block. Always work with well-ironed fabric; all pieces should be ironed before they are sewn together. Use a short needle, #7 to #10 (sizes #9 and #10 are the most popular) and an 18-inch length of #60 thread. Try various needles until you find one which is most comfortable for you. A long needle is not necessary because you are taking only a few stitches at a time, and a short needle is much easier to work with. Use white thread unless the patches are cut from very dark cloth.

To join two pieces, place them together with the right sides facing. Place a pin through both pieces at each end of the pencil line. Check on the back to make sure that the pins are *exactly* on the pencil lines. When sewing larger seams, place a pin every 1½ inches, removing pins as you sew past them. Always stitch on the sewing line, being very careful not to stitch into the margins at the corners.

Join the pieces with short, simple running stitches, taking a few back stitches at the beginning and end of

Place a pin through both pieces at each end of the pencil line.

Do not stitch into the margins at the corners.

Running Stitch.   *Back Stitch.*

each seam rather than a knot. If the seam is very long, it is a good idea to make a few back stitches at several places along the seam. Keep the seam as straight as possible along the pencil line. If you must sew two bias edges together, try to keep the thread taut enough so that the edges do not stretch as you sew them.

After you join two pieces together, press the seams flat to one side—not open. Open seams will weaken the quilt. Generally seams should all be pressed in the same direction, but darker pieces should not be pressed so that they fall under the lighter pieces since they may show through when the quilt is completed. All seams should be pressed before they are crossed with another seam. To keep seams from bunching, clip away excess fabric, if neccessary, at these crossing points.

As for using a sewing machine, old-time quilters frown on anything but the finest hand-sewing when piecing blocks. However, the sewing machine can serve a useful purpose when you are ready to set the blocks together—more about this below.

Setting the Quilt

After you have pieced the required number of blocks, lay them out to get the final effect before setting them together. Check to make sure that each block is turned the proper way.

You can now proceed with setting the blocks together. The best way is to join all the blocks of one row, sewing them with a ¼-inch seam. Continue joining blocks one row at a time. Some people feel that machine sewing here not only saves time but also strengthens the long seams. Others believe that it is easier to keep the pattern accurate and the corners matched if the work is done by hand. Some hand-sewers also find that the close machine stitches create difficulties later on when one gets ready to do the final quilt stitching.

Blocking the Quilt

The term ''blocking'' means keeping the edges straight on all sides of the quilt so that it will be a perfect rectangle when finished. The term applies to the quilt's divisions as well as to the entire quilt so the process of blocking is a continuous process from start to finish.

Right at the start it will help the blocking process if you have cut all of your pieces with the straight sides of the pattern parallel to the grain of the fabric because pieces cut on the bias have a tendency to pucker.

Pull the edges of the block straight with the fingers and pin the corners to the ironing board to hold them rigidly in place. Cover the block with a damp cloth and steam with a warm iron. Do not let the pressing cloth get dry. Iron the edges until they are perfectly straight and of equal measurements. The center is ironed last.

It is a good idea to iron each block after the sewing is completed. This means quite a lot of ironing, but it assures greater accuracy in the final measurements of all units. After the quilt is set together, it will need a final blocking before it is ready to be quilted to the filling and lining.

FINISHING THE QUILT

A completed quilt consists of three parts: the patchwork top, the filler or batting and the lining. The quilting stitches are used to firmly lock the patchwork top to both the lining and the batting in the middle. In primitive times, the three layers of covering were held together by stitches at a few main points, called the counter points. Next came interlacing diagonal lines, forming squares and diamonds, and gradually the decorative quilt stitching that we generally associate with early American quilts.

When the quilt is composed of squares, the quilting stitches cover the plain squares which alternate with the decorated ones, and this gives the effect of throwing the decorated part into more pronounced relief. These quilting stitches in the plain squares are sometimes in straight or diagonal lines and are usually planned to form a contrast to the pieced blocks. Thus, straight lines are chosen to contrast with a curving design, and curves and whirls are chosen when the main pattern is straight or geometrical.

Quilt Lining and Batting

You should choose the lining and batting for your quilt with the greatest care if you want your quilt to endure for years. It is false economy to use inferior materials; all of your time and painstaking stitches deserve the best! You may obtain cotton batting that is especially prepared for quilt filling. It comes in large sheets carefully folded and rolled. Perhaps you will need two packages, depending on the size of the quilt.

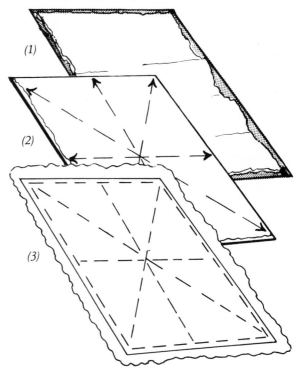

Finishing the quilt. (1) Placing batting on lining. (2) Basting batting to lining. (3) Basting marked top to batting and lining, through center and around edges.

The back of the quilt is made of lengths of soft material sewn together for correct width and length. It should be soft and loosely woven to make the quilt stitching easier. The over-all measurements should be 2 inches longer on each side to allow for binding when the quilt is completed. Carefully arrange the lining on a large flat surface, and fasten the corners with thumb tacks. Unroll the cotton batting and spread it out evenly on the lining, making sure there are no lumps or thin places that will make the quilting uneven.

Next, fasten the cotton batting securely to the lining with long basting stitches. Start in the center of the quilt, and sew toward the edge until you have a number of diagonal lines, as shown on page v.

Preparing the Quilt Top

Before the quilt top is joined to the batting and lining, the quilting pattern must be marked on the quilt top. There are many methods for marking the design on the fabric. The easiest method is to use a hard lead pencil. If the material is dark, use chalk or a piece of white soap trimmed to a thin point. If you sew directly on the pencil or chalk lines, they will not show when the work is finished.

You are now ready to lay the neatly ironed top in place over the lining and the cotton filling. Smooth it out and see that the edges correspond on all four sides. The three layers are now basted together just as you basted the first two—in diagonal lines from the center to the edges of the quilt.

The Quilting Stitch

The actual quilt stitching is a simple process for any one who can do any other form of needlework, but it does take a little practice. The first attempt should be in stitching straight lines, with curves and feathers coming later. It is helpful to use a practice piece of two squares of material with a layer of cotton in between. Try stitching the pieces together with a plain running stitch. You will soon learn the best method of pushing the needle in and out, and also the direction in which to sew. You will be sure to find that it is easier to sew *toward* you.

It is an interesting fact that many busy women who enjoy piecing blocks, but who do not care for the final quilting of the three layers, procure the services of professional quilters. There are church organizations, craft shops and private seamstresses who accept quilting at fair rates.

One reason why quilt stitching is often "farmed out" is that it is greatly simplified when done on a quilting frame, which is cumbersome. However, quilting can also be done successfully, if less rapidly, on a quilting hoop.

The purpose of the quilting stitch is to firmly lock the top of the quilt to both its filling and lining. Use a short Sharp needle, size #8 to 9. The choice of thread should be between #50 and 70, preferably white. It is important to start the quilting near the center of the frame because it is always easier to sew toward the body. To commence, make a knot at the end of the thread and bring the needle through to the top of the quilt, then pull gently but firmly and the knot will slip through the lower layer into the padding where it will not be seen. To finish off, make a single back stitch and run the thread through the padding. Cut, and the end will be lost.

Binding the Quilt

When the quilting is completed, trim the edges (except the lining extension if used for binding) on all four sides in an even line, being sure to remove any cotton that extends beyond the quilt's top. There are two methods for binding the edges: (1) Make use of the 2-inch extension of the back lining which was left on during the quilting process. Even it off all around, turn up an edge for a seam, and fold up over the top of the quilt. Sew in place with small hemming stitches in matching color thread. (2) Bind the edges with bias strips, if you are going to use a binding of different color or a scalloped border. Cut the bias strips 1 inch wide and sew them together. The binding is done by laying the bias strip along the outside edge of the quilt, and fitting the edges together so they match exactly. Sew the bias strip and all three layers together with a ¼-inch seam, using a running stitch. After the sewing is done, turn the quilt over and turn down the edges of the bias strip ¼ inch. Fold this over the back of the quilt and sew securely to the bottom layer with small hemming stitches.

EARLY AMERICAN PATCHWORK PATTERNS

WINDMILL QUILT

SIZE OF QUILT

This quilt, measuring 84 x 108 inches, is made up of sixty-three 12-inch pieced blocks set seven in width and nine in length.

COLOR CHART

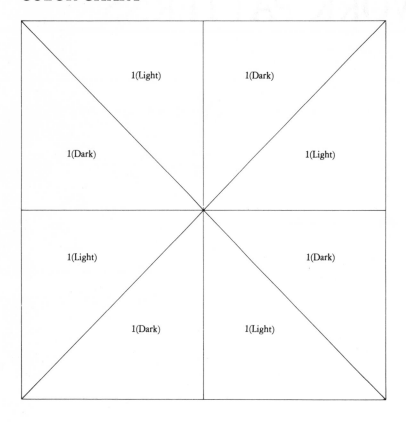

1(Light)

1(Dark)

1(Dark)

1(Light)

1(Light)

1(Dark)

1(Dark)

1(Light)

AMOUNT OF MATERIAL

Light . . . . 4¾ yards
Dark . . . . 4¾ yards

NUMBER OF PIECES TO BE CUT FOR EACH BLOCK

Piece No. 1 . . . . 4 Light
Piece No. 1 . . . . 4 Dark

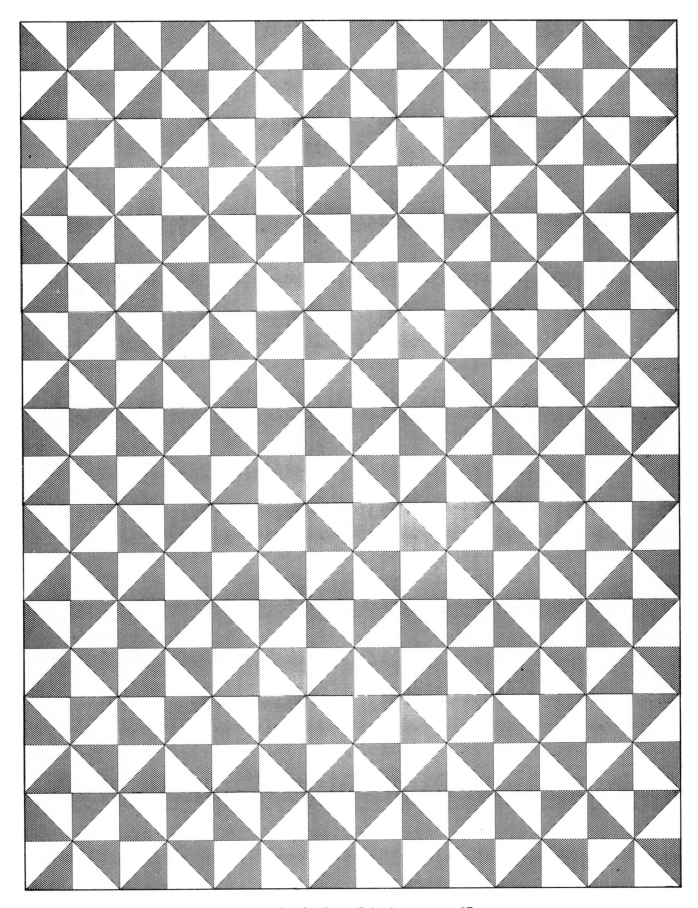

The template for this quilt is given on page 27.

EIGHT-POINTED STAR QUILT

SIZE OF QUILT

This quilt, measuring 84 x 96 inches, is made up of twenty-eight 12-inch pieced blocks and twenty-eight 12-inch plain blocks set seven in width and eight in length.

COLOR CHART

1(Dark)	2(Medium) 2(Light) 2(Light) 2(Medium)	1(Dark)
2(Light) 2(Medium) 2(Medium) 2(Light)	1(Light)	2(Light) 2(Medium) 2(Medium) 2(Light)
1(Dark)	2(Medium) 2(Light) 2(Light) 2(Medium)	1(Dark)

AMOUNT OF MATERIAL

Light	. . . .	5¼ yards
Dark	. . . .	2 yards
Medium	. . . .	1¼ yards

NUMBER OF PIECES TO BE CUT FOR EACH BLOCK

Piece No. 1	. . . .	1 Light
Piece No. 1	. . . .	4 Dark
Piece No. 2	. . . .	8 Light
Piece No. 2	. . . .	8 Medium

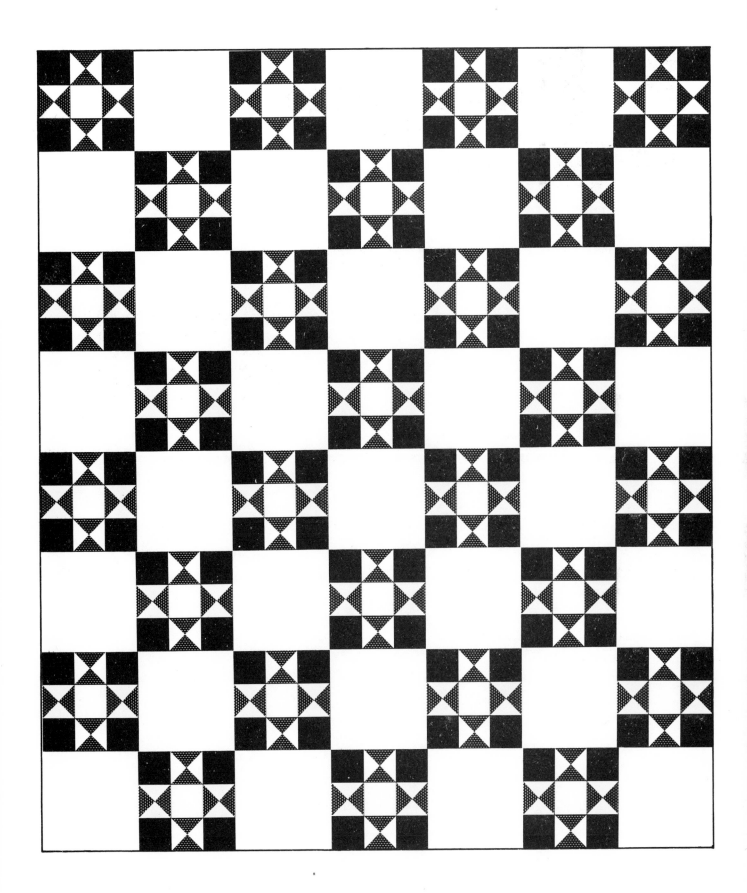

Templates for this quilt are given on page 30.

KITTY CORNER QUILT

SIZE OF QUILT

This quilt, measuring 84 x 108 inches, is made up of thirty-two 12-inch pieced blocks and thirty-one 12-inch plain blocks set seven in width and nine in length.

COLOR CHART

4(Light) 4(Light) 2(Dark) 4(Light) 4(Light)	5(Light) 1(Dark) 5(Light)	4(Light) 4(Light) 2(Dark) 4(Light) 4(Light)
5(Light) 1(Dark) 5(Light)	3(Light)	5(Light) 1(Dark) 5(Light)
4(Light) 4(Light) 2(Dark) 4(Light) 4(Light)	5(Light) 1(Dark) 5(Light)	4(Light) 4(Light) 2(Dark) 4(Light) 4(Light)

Amount of Material

Light . . . . 8½ yards
Dark . . . . 2¾ yards

NUMBER OF PIECES TO BE CUT FOR EACH BLOCK

Piece No. 1 . . . . 4 Dark
Piece No. 2 . . . . 4 Dark
Piece No. 3 . . . . 1 Light
Piece No. 4 . . . . 16 Light
Piece No. 5 . . . . 8 Light

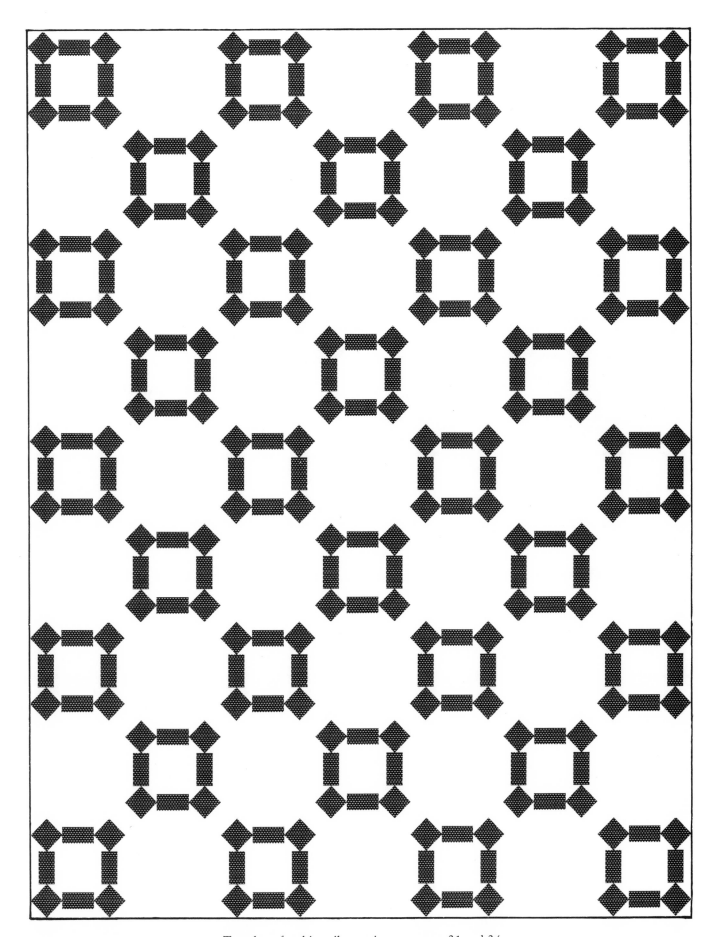

Templates for this quilt are given on pages 31 and 34.

STEEPLE CHASE QUILT

SIZE OF QUILT

This quilt, measuring 84 x 108 inches, is made up of thirty-two 12-inch "A" blocks and thirty-one 12-inch "B" blocks set seven in width and nine in length. The "B" block is the opposite of the "A" block.

"A" Block

"B" Block

AMOUNT OF MATERIAL

Light . . . . 7¾ yards
Dark . . . . 7¾ yards

NUMBER OF PIECES TO BE CUT FOR EACH "A" BLOCK

Piece No. 1 . . . . 2 Dark
Piece No. 2 . . . . 2 Light

NUMBER OF PIECES TO BE CUT FOR EACH "B" BLOCK

Piece No. 1 . . . . 2 Light
Piece No. 2 . . . . 2 Dark

COLOR CHART

"A" Block

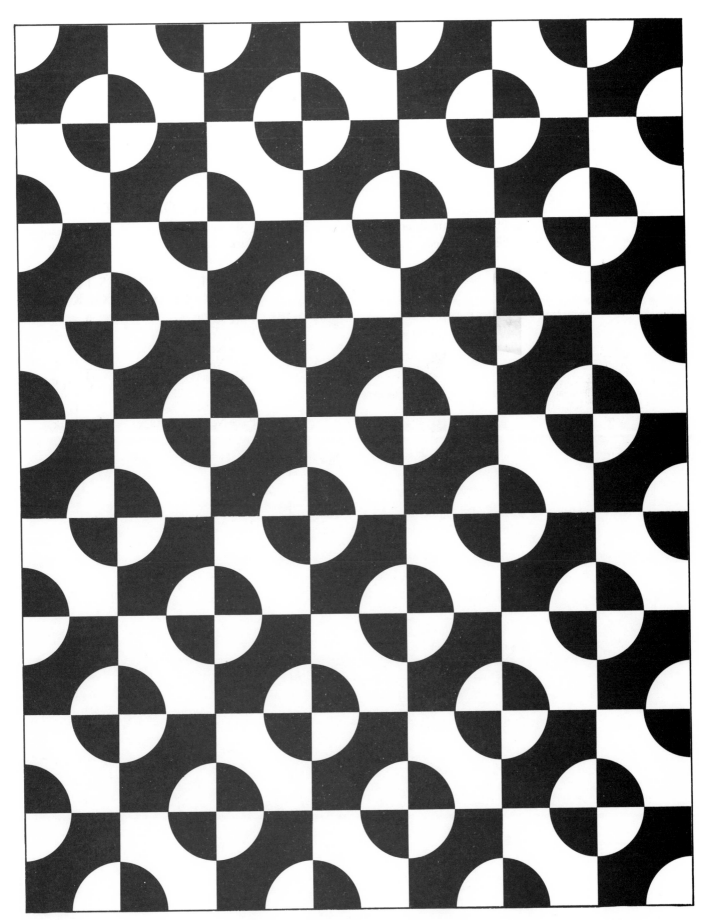

Templates for this quilt are given on page 35.

COMPASS QUILT

SIZE OF QUILT

This quilt, measuring 84 x 108 inches, is made up of sixty-three 12-inch pieced blocks set seven in width and nine in length.

COLOR CHART

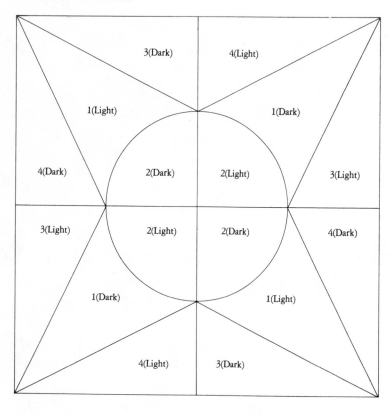

AMOUNT OF MATERIAL

Light . . . . 9¾ yards
Dark . . . . 9¾ yards

NUMBER OF PIECES TO BE CUT FOR EACH BLOCK

Piece No. 1 . . . . 2 Light
Piece No. 1 . . . . 2 Dark
Piece No. 2 . . . . 2 Light
Piece No. 2 . . . . 2 Dark
Piece No. 3 . . . . 2 Light
Piece No. 3 . . . . 2 Dark
Piece No. 4 . . . . 2 Light
Piece No. 4 . . . . 2 Dark

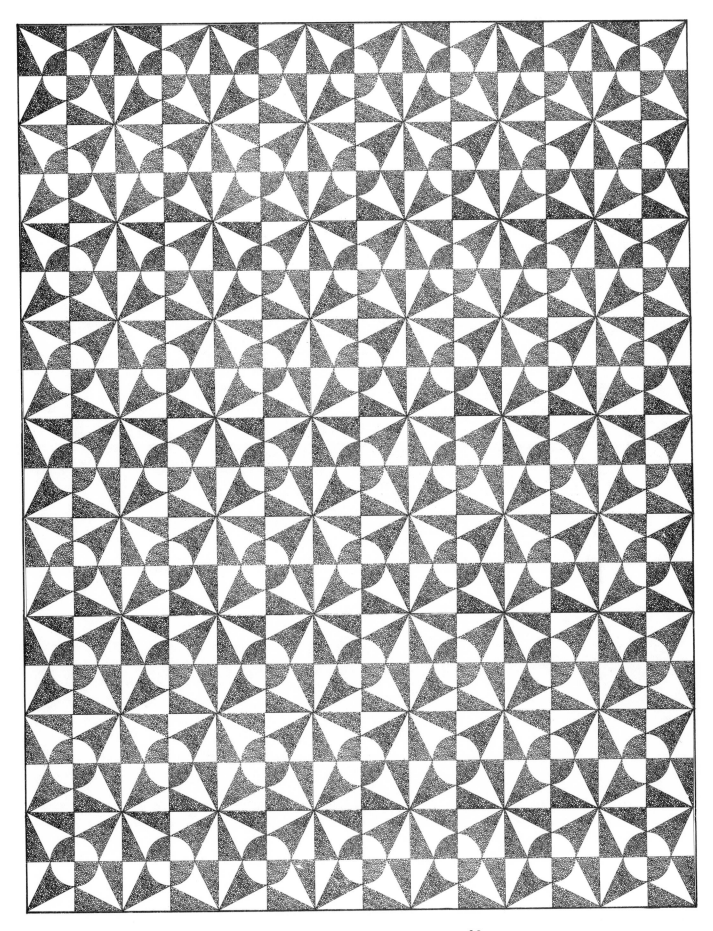

Templates for this quilt are given on page 38.

SHIP'S WHEEL QUILT

SIZE OF QUILT

This quilt, measuring 91 x 104 inches, is made up of fifty-six 13-inch pieced blocks set seven in width and eight in length.

COLOR CHART

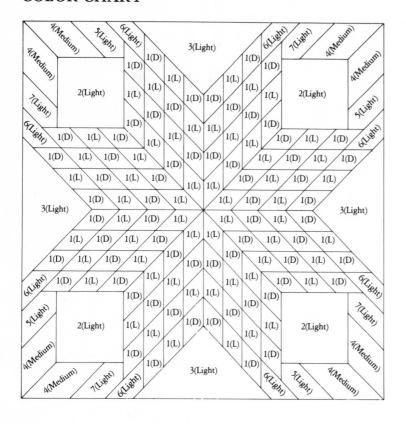

AMOUNT OF MATERIAL

Light	10⅓	yards
Medium	1¾	yards
Dark	5¼	yards

NUMBER OF PIECES TO BE CUT FOR EACH BLOCK

Piece No. 1	64	Dark
Piece No. 1	56	Light
Piece No. 2	4	Light
Piece No. 3	4	Light
Piece No. 4	8	Medium
Piece No. 5	4	Light
Piece No. 6	8	Light
Piece No. 7	4	Light

Templates for this quilt are given on page 39.

FLOWER BASKET QUILT

SIZE OF QUILT

This quilt, measuring 84 x 108 inches, is made up of sixty-three 12-inch pieced blocks seven in width and nine in length. The pieced square is made first; then the handle (piece #7) is appliquéd in place.

COLOR CHART

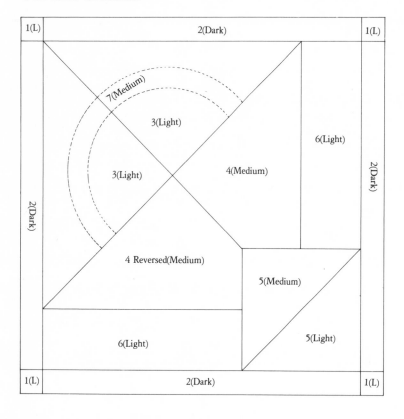

AMOUNT OF MATERIAL

Light	5	yards
Medium	7¼	yards
Dark	3	yards

NUMBER OF PIECES TO BE CUT FOR EACH BLOCK

Piece No. 1	4	Light
Piece No. 2	4	Dark
Piece No. 3	2	Light
Piece No. 4	1	Medium
Piece No. 4 Reversed	1	Medium
Piece No. 5	1	Medium
Piece No. 5	1	Light
Piece No. 6	2	Light
Piece No. 7	1	Medium

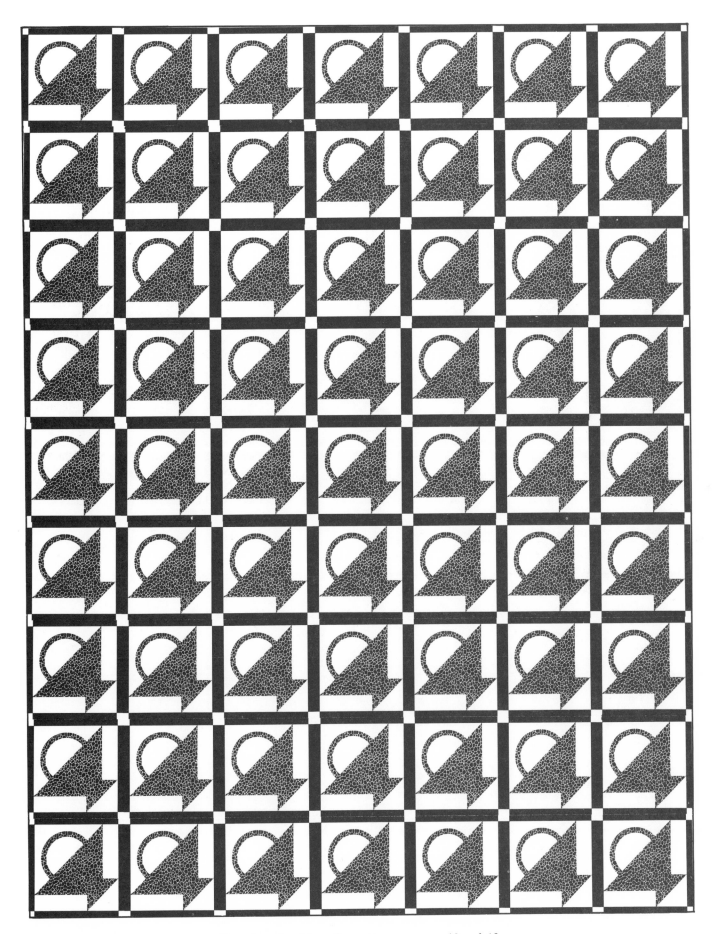

Templates for this quilt are given on pages 42 and 43.

15

TULIP QUILT

SIZE OF QUILT

This quilt, measuring 84 x 96 inches, is made up of fifty-six 12-inch pieced blocks set seven in width and eight in length. After the pieced square is completed, applique the stem onto the block. The stem may be cut from narrow-fold bias tape or strips of material about 3/8-inch wide, allowing for 1/8-inch turn-under.

AMOUNT OF MATERIAL

Light . . . . 7¼ yards
Medium . . . . 5 yards
Dark . . . . 2 yards

NUMBER OF PIECES TO BE CUT FOR EACH BLOCK

Piece No. 1 . . . . 5 Light
Piece No. 2 . . . . 2 Light
Piece No. 3 . . . . 18 Medium
Piece No. 3 . . . . 6 Dark
Piece No. 4 . . . . 8 Light
Piece No. 5 . . . . 1 Light
Piece No. 6 . . . . 1 Light
Piece No. 7 . . . . 1 Dark
Piece No. 8 . . . . 1 Light
Piece No. 9 . . . . 1 Dark
Piece No. 10 . . . . 1 Light
Piece No. 11 . . . . 1 Dark

COLOR CHART

Templates for this quilt are given on pages 46 and 47.

LOG CABIN QUILT

SIZE OF QUILT

This quilt, measuring 71¼ x 95 inches, is made up of forty-eight 11⅞-inch pieced blocks set six in width and eight in length.

COLOR CHART

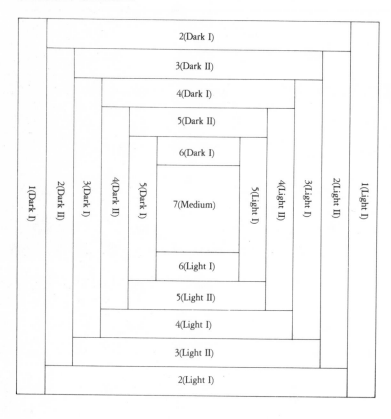

AMOUNT OF MATERIAL

Light I	4	yards
Light II	2⅔	yards
Medium	½	yard
Dark I	4	yards
Dark II	2⅔	yards

NUMBER OF PIECES TO BE CUT FOR EACH BLOCK

Piece No. 1	1	Dark I
Piece No. 1	1	Light I
Piece No. 2	1	Dark I
Piece No. 2	1	Dark II
Piece No. 2	1	Light I
Piece No. 2	1	Light II
Piece No. 3	1	Dark I
Piece No. 3	1	Dark II
Piece No. 3	1	Light I
Piece No. 3	1	Light II
Piece No. 4	1	Dark I
Piece No. 4	1	Dark II
Piece No. 4	1	Light I
Piece No. 4	1	Light II
Piece No. 5	1	Dark I
Piece No. 5	1	Dark II
Piece No. 5	1	Light I
Piece No. 5	1	Light II
Piece No. 6	1	Light I
Piece No. 6	1	Dark I
Piece No. 7	1	Medium

Templates for this quilt are given on page 50.

WILD GOOSE CHASE QUILT

SIZE OF QUILT

This quilt, measuring 84 x 96 inches, is made up of fifty-six 12-inch pieced blocks set seven in width and eight in length.

COLOR CHART

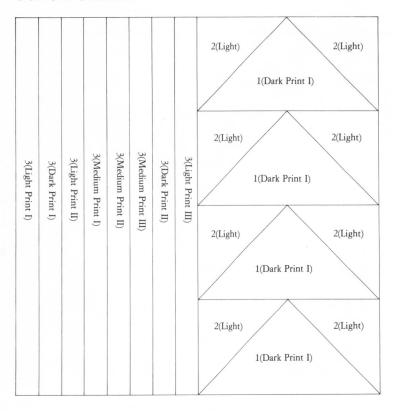

AMOUNT OF MATERIAL

Light	4½	yards
Light Print I	1	yard
Light Print II	1	yard
Light Print III	1	yard
Medium Print I	1	yard
Medium Print II	1	yard
Medium Print III	1	yard
Dark Print I	5½	yards
Dark Print II	1	yard

NUMBER OF PIECES TO BE CUT FOR EACH BLOCK

Piece No. 1	4	Dark Print I
Piece No. 2	8	Light
Piece No. 3	1	Light Print I
Piece No. 3	1	Light Print II
Piece No. 3	1	Light Print III
Piece No. 3	1	Medium Print I
Piece No. 3	1	Medium Print II
Piece No. 3	1	Medium Print III
Piece No. 3	1	Dark Print I
Piece No. 3	1	Dark Print II

Templates for this quilt are given on page 51.

DUCK'S-FOOT-IN-THE-MUD QUILT

SIZE OF QUILT

This quilt, measuring 84 x 108 inches, is made up of sixty-three 12-inch pieced blocks, set seven in width and nine in length.

COLOR CHART

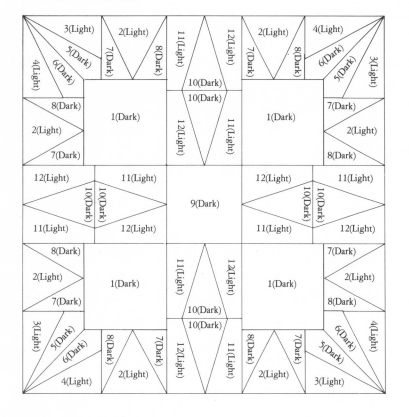

AMOUNT OF MATERIAL

Light . . . . 10¼ yards
Dark . . . . 9⅔ yards

NUMBER OF PIECES TO BE CUT FOR EACH BLOCK

Piece No. 1 . . . . 4 Dark
Piece No. 2 . . . . 8 Light
Piece No. 3 . . . . 4 Light
Piece No. 4 . . . . 4 Light
Piece No. 5 . . . . 4 Dark
Piece No. 6 . . . . 4 Dark
Piece No. 7 . . . . 8 Dark
Piece No. 8 . . . . 8 Dark
Piece No. 9 . . . . 1 Dark
Piece No. 10 . . . . 8 Dark
Piece No. 11 . . . . 8 Light
Piece No. 12 . . . . 8 Light

Templates for this quilt are given on page 54.

LITTLE RED SCHOOLHOUSE QUILT

SIZE OF QUILT

This quilt, measuring 84 x 108 inches, is made up of thirty-two 12-inch "A" blocks and thirty-one 12-inch "B" blocks, set seven in width and nine in length. The "B" block is the opposite of the "A" block.

"A" Block

"B" Block

COLOR CHART

1(Light)	2(Dark)								1(Light)
2(Dark)	17(Dark)	4(Light)	5(Dark)	4(Light)	3(Dark)				2(Dark)
	6(Light)	8(Dark)	7(Light)						
	11(Light)	12(Dark)	11(Light)	9(Dark)	10(Dark) 14(Light)				
					15(Light)	16(Dark)	15(Light)	16(Dark)	15(Light)
	13(Light)				14(Light)				
1(Light)	2(Dark)								1(Light)

"A" Block

AMOUNT OF MATERIAL

Light . . . . 6⅓ yards
Dark . . . . 6⅓ yards

NUMBER OF PIECES TO BE CUT FOR EACH "A" BLOCK

Piece No. 1 . . . . 4 Light
Piece No. 2 . . . . 4 Dark
Piece No. 3 . . . . 1 Dark
Piece No. 4 . . . . 2 Light
Piece No. 5 . . . . 1 Dark
Piece No. 6 . . . . 1 Light
Piece No. 7 . . . . 1 Light
Piece No. 8 . . . . 1 Dark
Piece No. 9 . . . . 1 Dark
Piece No. 10 . . . . 1 Dark
Piece No. 11 . . . . 2 Light
Piece No. 12 . . . . 1 Dark
Piece No. 13 . . . . 1 Light
Piece No. 14 . . . . 2 Light
Piece No. 15 . . . . 3 Light
Piece No. 16 . . . . 2 Dark
Piece No. 17 . . . . 1 Dark

NUMBER OF PIECES TO BE CUT FOR EACH "B" BLOCK

Piece No. 1 . . . . 4 Dark
Piece No. 2 . . . . 4 Light
Piece No. 3 . . . . 1 Light
Piece No. 4 . . . . 2 Dark
Piece No. 5 . . . . 1 Light
Piece No. 6 . . . . 1 Dark
Piece No. 7 . . . . 1 Dark
Piece No. 8 . . . . 1 Light
Piece No. 9 . . . . 1 Light
Piece No. 10 . . . . 1 Light
Piece No. 11 . . . . 2 Dark
Piece No. 12 . . . . 1 Light
Piece No. 13 . . . . 1 Dark
Piece No. 14 . . . . 2 Dark
Piece No. 15 . . . . 3 Dark
Piece No. 16 . . . . 2 Light
Piece No. 17 . . . . 1 Light

Templates for this quilt are given on pages 55 and 58.

PATTERN PIECES FOR
WINDMILL QUILT

Allow for all seams when cutting.

WINDMILL
Piece No. 1

PATTERN PIECES FOR
EIGHT-POINTED STAR QUILT

Allow for all seams when cutting.

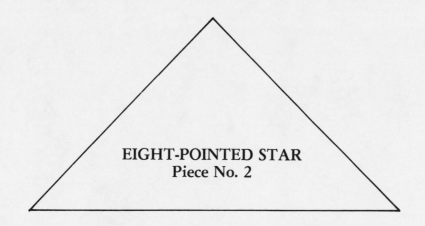

EIGHT-POINTED STAR
Piece No. 1

EIGHT-POINTED STAR
Piece No. 2

PATTERN PIECES FOR
KITTY CORNER QUILT

Allow for all seams when cutting.

KITTY CORNER
Piece No. 1

KITTY CORNER
Piece No. 3

PATTERN PIECES FOR
KITTY CORNER QUILT

Allow for all seams when cutting.

KITTY CORNER
Piece No. 2

KITTY CORNER
Piece No. 4

KITTY CORNER
Piece No. 5

PATTERN PIECES FOR
STEEPLE CHASE QUILT

Allow for all seams when cutting.

STEEPLE CHASE
Piece No. 1

Place on fold

STEEPLE CHASE
Piece No. 2

Place on fold

PATTERN PIECES FOR
COMPASS QUILT

Allow for all seams when cutting.

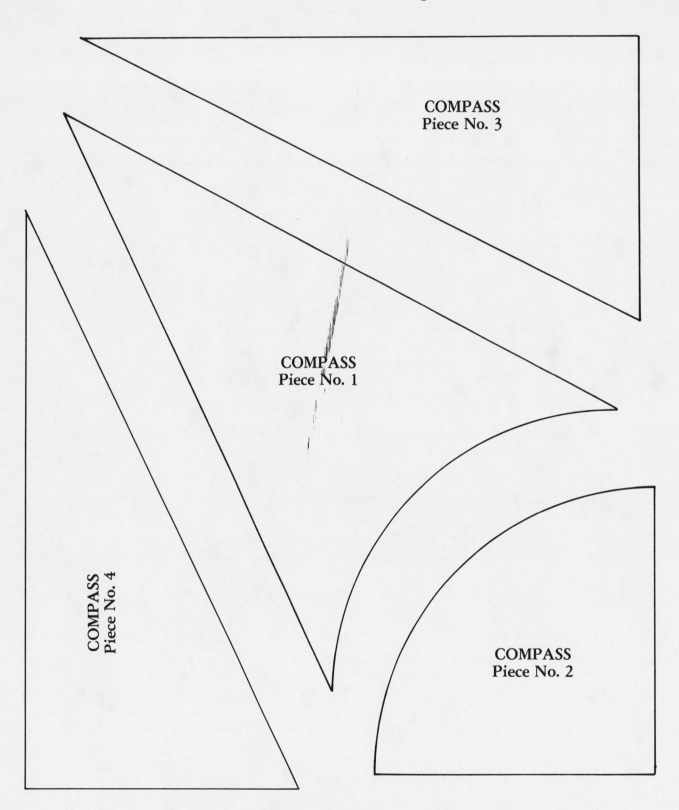

COMPASS
Piece No. 3

COMPASS
Piece No. 1

COMPASS
Piece No. 4

COMPASS
Piece No. 2

PATTERN PIECES FOR
SHIP'S WHEEL QUILT

Allow for all seams when cutting.

SHIP'S WHEEL
Piece No. 2

SHIP'S WHEEL
Piece No. 7

SHIP'S WHEEL
Piece No. 5

SHIP'S WHEEL
Piece No. 1

SHIP'S WHEEL
Piece No. 6

SHIP'S WHEEL
Piece No. 3

SHIP'S WHEEL
Piece No. 4

PATTERN PIECES FOR
FLOWER BASKET QUILT

Allow for all seams when cutting.

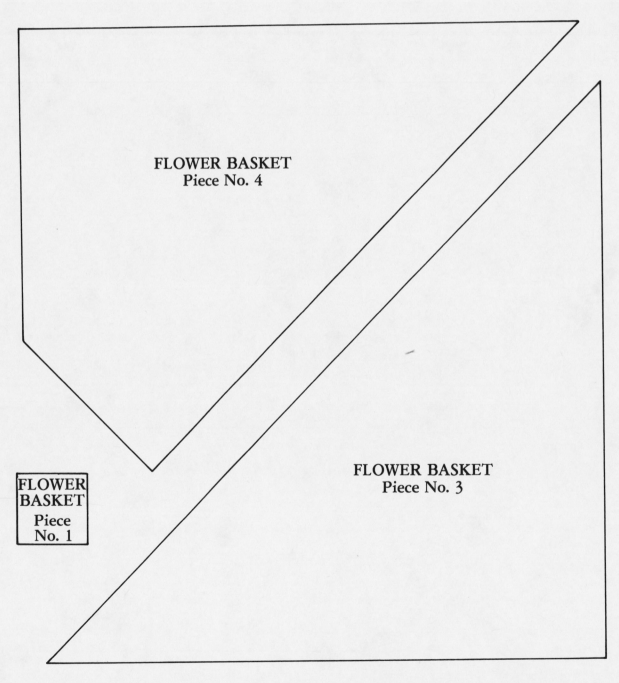

FLOWER BASKET
Piece No. 2

Place on fold

FLOWER BASKET
Piece No. 4

FLOWER BASKET
Piece
No. 1

FLOWER BASKET
Piece No. 3

PATTERN PIECES FOR
FLOWER BASKET QUILT

Allow for all seams when cutting.

FLOWER BASKET
Piece No. 7

FLOWER BASKET
Piece No. 5

FLOWER BASKET
Piece No. 6

PATTERN PIECES FOR
TULIP QUILT

Allow for all seams when cutting.

TULIP
Piece No. 4

TULIP
Piece No. 2

TULIP
Piece No. 3

TULIP
Piece No. 10

TULIP
Piece No. 5

TULIP
Piece No. 1

PATTERN PIECES FOR
TULIP QUILT

Allow for all seams when cutting.

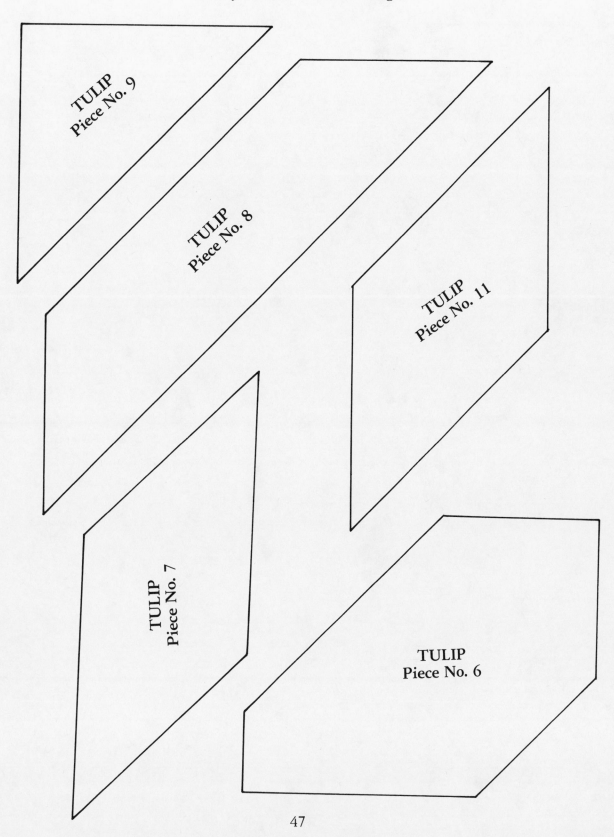

TULIP
Piece No. 9

TULIP
Piece No. 8

TULIP
Piece No. 11

TULIP
Piece No. 7

TULIP
Piece No. 6

PATTERN PIECES FOR
LOG CABIN QUILT

Allow for all seams when cutting.

LOG CABIN
Piece No. 5

LOG CABIN
Piece No. 6

LOG CABIN
Piece No. 4

LOG CABIN
Piece No. 2

LOG CABIN
Piece No. 3

LOG CABIN
Piece No. 7

*Place
on fold*

*Place
on fold*

LOG CABIN
Piece No. 1

PATTERN PIECES FOR
WILD GOOSE CHASE QUILT

Allow for all seams when cutting.

PATTERN PIECES FOR
DUCK'S-FOOT-IN-THE-MUD QUILT

Allow for all seams when cutting.

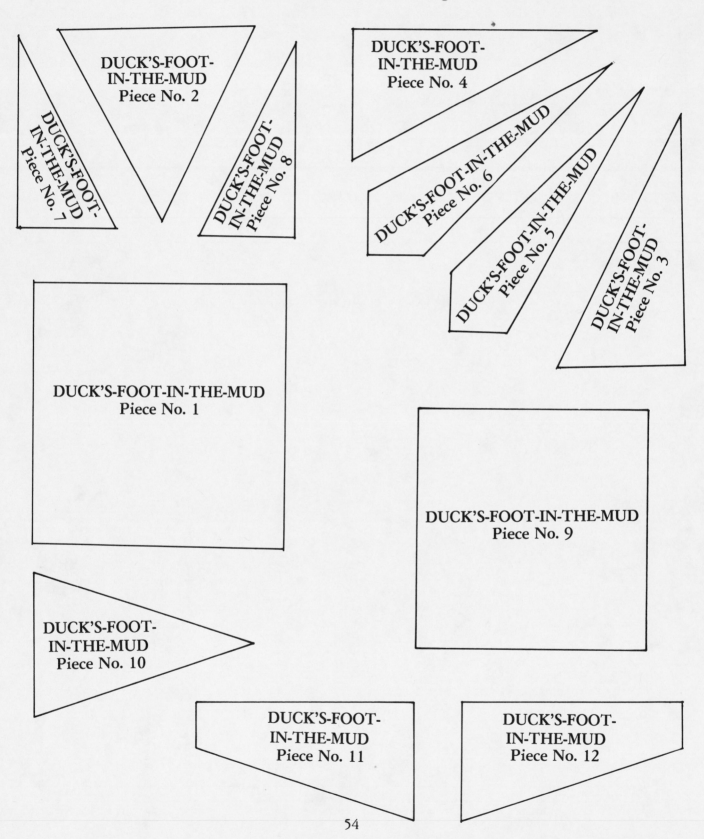

DUCK'S-FOOT-IN-THE-MUD
Piece No. 2

DUCK'S-FOOT-IN-THE-MUD
Piece No. 7

DUCK'S-FOOT-IN-THE-MUD
Piece No. 8

DUCK'S-FOOT-IN-THE-MUD
Piece No. 4

DUCK'S-FOOT-IN-THE-MUD
Piece No. 6

DUCK'S-FOOT-IN-THE-MUD
Piece No. 5

DUCK'S-FOOT-IN-THE-MUD
Piece No. 3

DUCK'S-FOOT-IN-THE-MUD
Piece No. 1

DUCK'S-FOOT-IN-THE-MUD
Piece No. 9

DUCK'S-FOOT-IN-THE-MUD
Piece No. 10

DUCK'S-FOOT-IN-THE-MUD
Piece No. 11

DUCK'S-FOOT-IN-THE-MUD
Piece No. 12

PATTERN PIECES FOR
LITTLE RED SCHOOLHOUSE QUILT

Allow for all seams when cutting.

LITTLE RED SCHOOLHOUSE
Piece No. 5

LITTLE
RED
SCHOOL
HOUSE
Piece No. 4

LITTLE RED SCHOOLHOUSE
Piece No. 3

LITTLE RED SCHOOLHOUSE
Piece No. 7

LITTLE RED
SCHOOLHOUSE
Piece No. 6

LITTLE RED
SCHOOLHOUSE
Piece No. 1

LITTLE RED SCHOOLHOUSE
Piece No. 8

Place on fold

LITTLE RED SCHOOLHOUSE
Piece No. 2

PATTERN PIECES FOR
LITTLE RED SCHOOLHOUSE QUILT

Allow for all seams when cutting.

LITTLE RED SCHOOLHOUSE
Piece No. 9

LITTLE RED SCHOOLHOUSE
Piece No. 10

LITTLE RED SCHOOLHOUSE
Piece No. 11

LITTLE RED SCHOOLHOUSE
Piece No. 12

LITTLE RED SCHOOLHOUSE
Piece No. 13

LITTLE RED SCHOOLHOUSE
Piece No. 14

LITTLE RED SCHOOLHOUSE
Piece No. 15

LITTLE RED SCHOOLHOUSE
Piece No. 16

LITTLE RED SCHOOLHOUSE
Piece No. 17